What Do You Call a Group of Alligators?

And Other Reptile and Amphibian Groups

EMMA NATHAN

BLACKBIRCH PRESS, INC.

WOODBRIDGE, CONNECTICUT

Published by Blackbirch Press, Inc.
260 Amity Road
Woodbridge, CT 06525
web site: http://www.blackbirch.com
e-mail: staff@blackbirch.com

Printed in Singapore

10 9 8 7 6 5 4 3 2 1

Photo Credits
Cover, pages 3, 9, 11, 19, 21: ©Photodisc; page 4: ©Mickey Gibson/Animals Animals; pages 5, 7, 10, 12: ©Corel Corporation; page 6: ©Martha Cooper/Peter Arnold, Inc.; pages 8, 22: ©Michael Fogden/Animals Animals; pages 13, 15, 17: ©PhotoSpin, Inc.; page 14: ©Fabio Colombini/Animals Animals; page 16: ©Tom McHugh/Photo Researchers, Inc.; page 17: ©Photospin; page 18: ©Zig Leszczynski/ Animals Animals; page 20: ©Gregory G. Dimijian/Photo Researchers, Inc.

Library of Congress Cataloging-in-Publication Data
Nathan, Emma.
        What do you call a group of alligators?: and other reptile and amphibian groups / by Emma Nathan.
        p. cm.—(What do you call a—)
        Includes index.
        Summary: Examines the habits of various reptiles and amphibians and explains what you call groups of them such as a quiver of cobras, a bask of crocodiles, and a knot of toads.
        ISBN 1-56711-358-3 (hardcover : acid-free paper)
        1. Reptiles—Miscellanea—Juvenile literature. 2.Amphibians—Miscellanea—Juvenile literature. 3. English language—Collective nouns—Juvenile literature. [1. Reptiles—Miscellanea. 2. Amphibians—Miscellanea. 3. English language—Collective nouns. 4. Questions and answers.] I.Title.
QL644.2 .N3484 2000   00-009057
597.9—dc21

Contents

What do you call a group of cobras?   3

What do you call a group of crocodiles?   5

What do you call a group of toads?   7

What do you call a group of turtles?   9

What do you call a group of alligators? 11

What do you call a group of frogs?   13

What do you call a group of rattlesnakes?   15

What do you call a group of salamanders?   17

What do you call a group of lizards? 19

What do you call a group of vipers? 21

Glossary   23

For More Information   23

Index   24

What do you call a group of cobras?

··WHAT DO YOU KNOW?··

Make Me Quiver

A quiver of cobras is something not too many people want to see! That's because cobras are among the most dangerous snakes in the world. Roughly 1 out of every 10 people who are bitten will die. The king cobra is the largest poisonous snake in the world. It can measure up to 15 feet (4.6 meters). A cobra can spit its poison in addition to biting. Some king cobras have been known to spit accurately from up to 12 feet (3.6 meters) away!

What do you call a group of crocodiles**?**

Crocodile Style

Most crocodiles prefer to live on their own. During breeding season, however, males and females may live together in groups. Large, shallow bodies of water—rivers, lakes, marshes, and swamps—make the best habitats for crocodiles. Although these large reptiles swim and feed in the water, they do crawl up on land to breed and to warm themselves in the sun.

A group of crocodiles is called a float or a bask.

What do you call a group of toads?

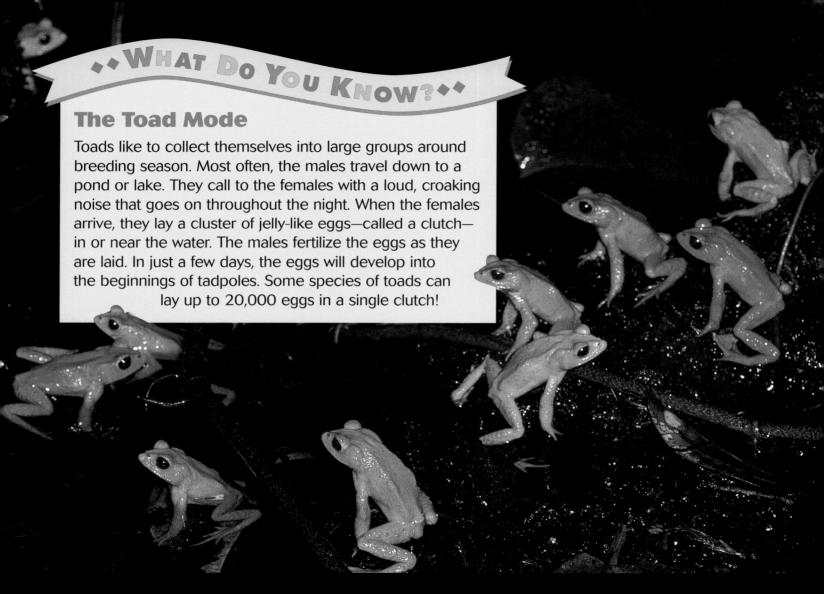

The Toad Mode

Toads like to collect themselves into large groups around breeding season. Most often, the males travel down to a pond or lake. They call to the females with a loud, croaking noise that goes on throughout the night. When the females arrive, they lay a cluster of jelly-like eggs—called a clutch—in or near the water. The males fertilize the eggs as they are laid. In just a few days, the eggs will develop into the beginnings of tadpoles. Some species of toads can lay up to 20,000 eggs in a single clutch!

A group of toads is called a knot.

What do you call a group of turtles?

•• WHAT DO YOU KNOW? ••

The Tale of the Bale

Female sea turtles like to gather together to lay their eggs on a sandy beach. Many sea turtle species return to lay their eggs in the exact same location every year. Before mating, land and sea turtles go through a period of courtship. After mating, a female can lay anywhere from 1 to 100 eggs. In general, turtles have long lifespans. Many turtles can live from 30 to 50 years in the wild.

What do you call a group of alligators**?**

Congregation Station

Alligators are solitary (live alone) for most of the year. During breeding season, however, groups of alligators gather together. Bulls (males) congregate in shallow water and roar loudly to attract females. After mating, the females crawl onto land and lay their eggs in large nests they have built with rotting plants. After 3 to 4 months, hatchlings emerge from their leathery eggs. Then they are carried in their mother's mouth to the nearby water.

What do you call a group of frogs?

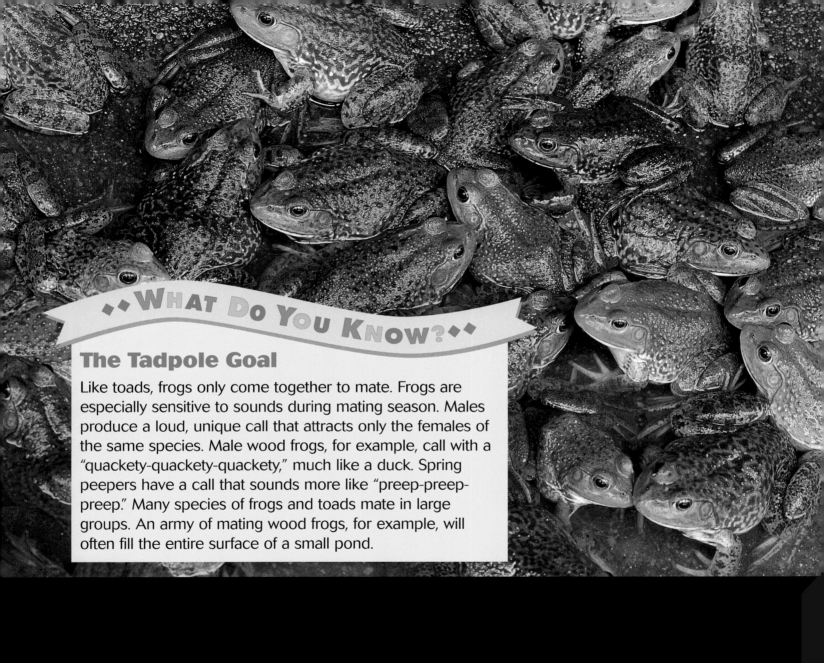

The Tadpole Goal

Like toads, frogs only come together to mate. Frogs are especially sensitive to sounds during mating season. Males produce a loud, unique call that attracts only the females of the same species. Male wood frogs, for example, call with a "quackety-quackety-quackety," much like a duck. Spring peepers have a call that sounds more like "preep-preep-preep." Many species of frogs and toads mate in large groups. An army of mating wood frogs, for example, will often fill the entire surface of a small pond.

What do you call a group of rattlesnakes?

Snakes with the Shakes

Rattlesnakes are not often seen in large groups, except when breeding grounds or nests are shared. All 28 species of rattlesnakes bear live young. Most often, they give birth to 12 or 15 snakelets at a time. All species except one have a rattle. A rattlesnake's rattle is really small, hollow pieces of keratin, a material similar to human nails or hair. Keratin makes up a snake's skin. Every time a snake molts (sheds its skin), another hollow segment of keratin is added to the tail. A rattlesnake uses the rattling sound to warn enemies that it is dangerous.

What do you call a group of salamanders?

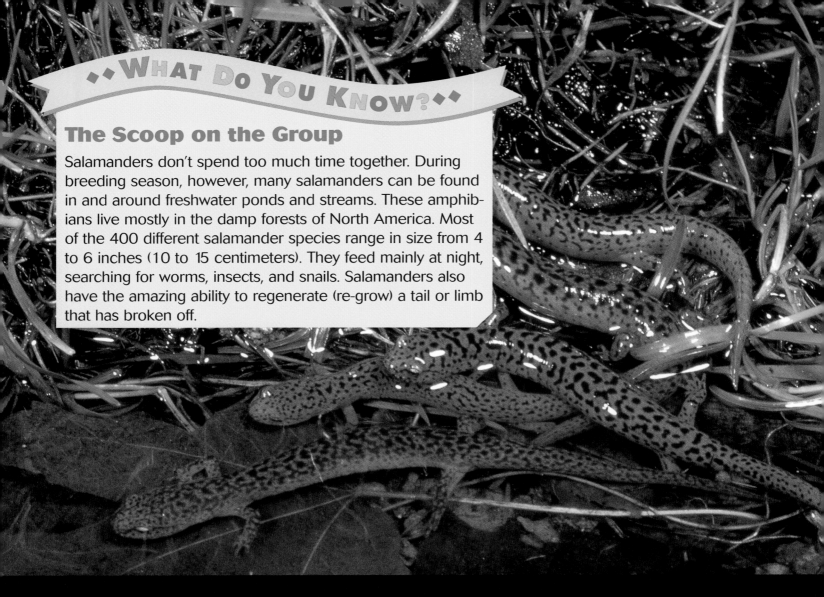

The Scoop on the Group

Salamanders don't spend too much time together. During breeding season, however, many salamanders can be found in and around freshwater ponds and streams. These amphibians live mostly in the damp forests of North America. Most of the 400 different salamander species range in size from 4 to 6 inches (10 to 15 centimeters). They feed mainly at night, searching for worms, insects, and snails. Salamanders also have the amazing ability to regenerate (re-grow) a tail or limb that has broken off.

A group of salamanders is called a group.

What do you call a group of lizards?

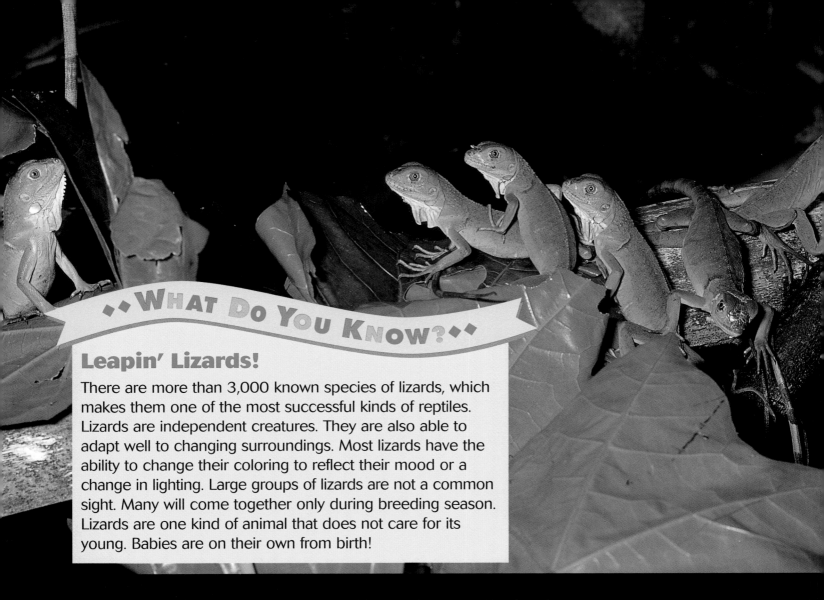

Leapin' Lizards!

There are more than 3,000 known species of lizards, which makes them one of the most successful kinds of reptiles. Lizards are independent creatures. They are also able to adapt well to changing surroundings. Most lizards have the ability to change their coloring to reflect their mood or a change in lighting. Large groups of lizards are not a common sight. Many will come together only during breeding season. Lizards are one kind of animal that does not care for its young. Babies are on their own from birth!

A group of lizards is called a leap.

What do you call a group of vipers❓

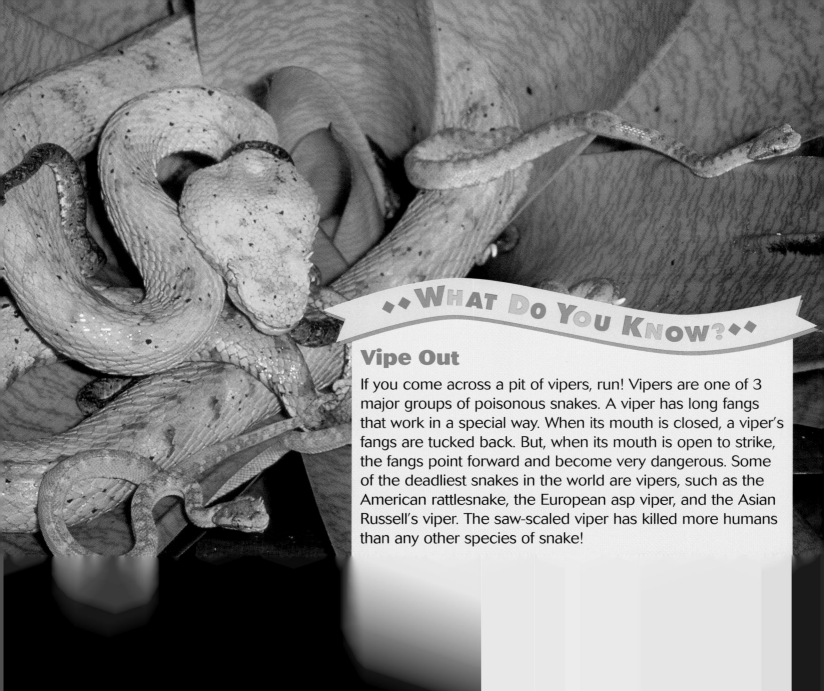

Vipe Out

If you come across a pit of vipers, run! Vipers are one of 3 major groups of poisonous snakes. A viper has long fangs that work in a special way. When its mouth is closed, a viper's fangs are tucked back. But, when its mouth is open to strike, the fangs point forward and become very dangerous. Some of the deadliest snakes in the world are vipers, such as the American rattlesnake, the European asp viper, and the Asian Russell's viper. The saw-scaled viper has killed more humans than any other species of snake!

Glossary

Adapt—to change in some way to fit in to a new situation.

Breed—to mate and produce young.

Clutch—a group of eggs, or young born at the same time.

Courtship—attempts by one living thing to win the love and affection of another living thng.

Habitat—the place and natural conditions in which a plant or animal lives.

Keratin—protein that forms some parts of the body, such as hair and nails.

Molt—to shed an outer covering of skin, fur, or feathers so that a new one can grow.

Solitary—single; spending a lot of time alone.

Species—one of the groups into which a plant or animal is divided, according to shared characteristics.

Unique—one of a kind.

For More Information

Books

Dossenbach, Hans. *Beware, We are Poisonous!* Woodbridge, CT: Blackbirch Press, Inc., 1993.

Dudley, Karen. *Alligators and Crocodiles* (The Untamed World). Chatham, NJ: Raintree/Steck Vaughn, 1998.

Gerholdt, James. *Frogs* (Amazing Amphibians). Minneapolis, MN: Abdo Publishing Company, 1994.

Julivert, Maria. *The Fascinating World of Snakes.* Hauppauge, NY: Barron's Juveniles, 1993.

Ricciuti, Edward. *Amphibians* (Our Living World). Woodbridge, CT: Blackbirch Press, Inc., 1994.

Web Sites

Crocodiles

Learn interesting information about each member of the crocodile family, including characteristics, body parts, and behaviors—www.pbs.org/wgbh/nova/crocs

International Rattlesnake Museum

Find fascinating facts about rattlesnake fangs, rattles, bites, and behavior—www.rattlesnake.com/info/info.html

Index

Alligators, 11, 12
Army, 14

Bale, 10
Breeding season, 6, 8,
    12, 20
Bulls, 12

Clutch, 8
Cobras, 3, 4
Congregation, 12
Crocodiles, 5, 6

Eggs, 8, 10, 12
European asp, 22

Fangs, 22
Float, 6
Frogs, 13, 14
    Wood Frogs, 14

Group, 18

Hatchlings, 12

Keratin, 16
King cobra, 4
Knot, 8

Leap, 20
Lizards, 19, 20

Molting, 16

Nest, 12, 16, 22

Pit, 22
Poison, 4, 22

Quiver, 4

Rattlesnakes, 15, 16,
    22
Rhumba, 16
Russell's viper, 22

Salamanders, 17, 18

Snakelets, 16
Saw-scaled viper, 22
Spring peepers, 14

Tadpole, 8, 14
Toads, 7, 8
Turtles, 9, 10

Vipers, 21, 22